The Northwest Twelve Days of Christmas

Gina Marie Mammano Illustrated by Cynthia Kremsner

PELICAN PUBLISHING COMPANY
GRETNA 2018

ISBN: 9781455623297
Ebook ISBN: 9781455623303

Printed in Malaysia

Published by Pelican Publishing Company, Inc.
1000 Burmaster Street, Gretna, Louisiana 70053
www.pelicanpub.com

To Ginny and John and all the children their good hearts nourish and care for

**On the first day of Christmas,
my hipster gave to me**

a grunge jam near the Salish Sea.

On the second day of Christmas,
my hipster gave to me two tanoak trees

and a grunge jam near the Salish Sea.

On the third day of Christmas,
my hipster gave to me
three flannel shirts,
two tanoak trees,
and a grunge jam near the Salish Sea.

On the fourth day of Christmas,
my hipster gave to me
four ferry horns,

three flannel shirts,
two tanoak trees,
and a grunge jam near the Salish Sea.

On the fifth day of Christmas,
my hipster gave to me
five weeks of rain!
four ferry horns,
three flannel shirts,
two tanoak trees,

and a grunge jam near the Salish Sea.

On the sixth day of Christmas,
my hipster gave to me
six salmon swimming,
"Five Weeks of Rain!"

four ferry horns,
three flannel shirts,
two tanoak trees,
and a grunge jam near the Salish Sea.

On the seventh day of Christmas, my hipster gave to me

seven Sasquatch swinging,
six salmon swimming,
"Five Weeks of Rain!"

four ferry horns,
three flannel shirts,
two tanoak trees,
and a grunge jam near the Salish Sea.

On the eighth day of Christmas,
my hipster gave to me
eight orcas clicking,
seven Sasquatch swinging,
six salmon swimming,
Five Weeks of Rain!

four ferry horns,
three flannel shirts,
two tanoak trees,
and a grunge jam near the Salish Sea.

On the ninth day of Christmas,
my hipster gave to me
nine keyboards clacking,
eight orcas clicking,
seven Sasquatch swinging,
six salmon swimming,

♪ Five Weeks of Rain! ♫

four ferry horns,
three flannel shirts,
two tanoak trees,
and a grunge jam near
the Salish Sea.

On the tenth day of Christmas,
my hipster gave to me
ten Braeburns blushing,
nine keyboards clacking,
eight orcas clicking,
seven Sasquatch swinging,
six salmon swimming,

♪ Five Weeks of Rain! ♫

four ferry horns,
three flannel shirts,
two tanoak trees,
and a grunge jam near the Salish Sea.

On the eleventh day of Christmas,
my hipster gave to me
eleven sea hawks rushing,
ten Braeburns blushing,

nine keyboards clacking,
eight orcas clicking,
seven Sasquatch swinging,
six salmon swimming,

"Five Weeks of Rain!"

four ferry horns,
three flannel shirts,
two tanoak trees,
and a grunge jam near the Salish Sea.

On the twelfth day of Christmas,
my hipster gave to me
twelve cups of coffee,
eleven sea hawks rushing,
ten Braeburns blushing,
nine keyboards clacking,
eight orcas clicking,
seven Sasquatch swinging,
six salmon
swimming,

"Five Weeks of Rain!"

four ferry horns,
three flannel shirts,
two tanoak trees, and a

grunge jam near the Salish Sea.

HIPSTR

The

End

Glossary

Braeburns—Crispy, streaky-red, tart-sweet apples picked in the winter in places such as Washington State.

grunge—A kind of rock music based in Seattle in the 1980s and 1990s that included dirty, distorted guitar sounds and groaning, heartfelt vocals made popular by groups such as Nirvana, Soundgarden, and Pearl Jam.

hipster—A young man or woman, sometimes wearing a beard, vest, and fedora hat, or pink hair, tattoos, and vintage thrift-store clothes, who wants to do his or her own thing, sometimes in a group of hipsters who like to do their own things together.

orcas—Also known as killer whales, orcas are actually black and white oceanic dolphins with teeth. They produce clicking sounds for navigation and communication.

Salish Sea—A collection of coastal waterways named after a tribe whose name simply means "the people" and that includes the Puget Sound, a couple of straits, and lots of salmon!

Sasquatch—Also known as "Bigfoot," this legendary creature is big, hairy, and supposedly part human, with as many tales about him as there are trees in the Pacific Northwest.

sea hawks—A nickname for ospreys, skuas, and, when the words are stuck together, a famous football team in Seattle.

tanoak tree—An evergreen in the beech tree family, closely related to the oak tree. Its valuable acorns were used by many coastal tribes, including the Karuk, Yurok, Klamath, and Hoopa, among others.